PoHymns

Saurabh Walia

Presentation by *BookLeaf Publishing*

Web: www.bookleafpub.com

E-mail: info@bookleafpub.com

ISBN:9789363313774

First edition 2025

DEDICATION

Dedicated to my parents, sister, niece and all
my near and dear ones.

Dedicated to my Incredible India.

Dedicated to everyone out there with a head full
of dreams and a heart full of hope.

ACKNOWLEDGEMENT

Thank you to my superheroes–my parents, Mrs. Pratibha Walia and Mr. Raj Kumar Walia, who have always inspired me to do good in life. Heartfelt thanks to my bravely beautiful sister, Mrs. Surbhi Walia, who pushes me to express more, write more, and embrace more; it's because of her that this book has seen the light of the day. A big, sweet thank you to my little munchkin, my amazing niece Samayra, whose innocence and sprouting spirit have embellished my experiences and hence my expressions. To my dear friends for always having my back and for being the reason to do better and bigger things in life. Would like to acknowledge and thank all my Gurus, family members, and colleagues who have all contributed to shaping the Me, who I am, and for being the melody to my life lessons. I would also like to thank the creator for choosing India as my home because, amidst all its struggles and successes, India has been a perennial source of inspiration for me and my literary works.

PREFACE

"What is this life if, full of care, we have no time to stand and stare." As a kid, I read this line somewhere, and since then it has been the cornerstone of my life. We all have our own complex stories, mixed with all sorts of problems, moments of gratification, struggles, serenity, and whatnot. But how many times do we actually look life in the eye and just observe its clockwork? We keep rushing and gushing, and hence often forget to embrace the tiny sprouts of glee and glam that life offers us every now and then that actually define the Tree of Our Life. Hope, strength, wisdom, and happiness–they all work in tandem with each other at all times in life. Having a heart full of dreams and a head full of hope is what makes us humane. Ups and downs, highs and lows, are part and parcel of life, but learning to dance in the rain while going through the storm and conditioning oneself for the best while going through the worst is what defines how one lives. While the journey is full of jolts and bumps and all sorts of rollercoasters, one needs to find a reason to cling onto their seat, hold their post, and keep swinging, keep hoping, and keep inspiring (life).

Music, movies, art, songs, literary musings, travelling, aspiring to be better and brighter–all this has had a profound impact on shaping the human as well as the poet within me. Hence, the writings reflect all the above and much more in an ebullient manner. It is said, "When the going gets tough, the tough get going." Being a stalwart supporter of the above emotion, the content of the book is entwined around the same. The purpose of the book is to ignite a spark of hope and sprout a green tree of self-help and dreams in the hearts of readers despite the epiphanies of life.

With the motto 'Vasudev Kutumbakam' (The world is One Family) as a pivotal element of the book, it aims to spread the message of brotherhood, unity, and compassion. It's like having bigger goals and pursuing them with a bigger team, leading to bigger moments, and memories in life.

For questions that may come up from all and every direction, answers are generally found by looking inside and around and by finding your real self, embracing your true spirit, and tirelessly enduring to make the world a better place. All this is in the form of a few rhyming verses, and you have *PoHymns*!

"Promise your potential to be as promising as the creator would have wanted it to be, and everything else shall be taken care of."

The Pier

The night is strong, so the knight should be
stronger,
For the clouds are dark, so the star needs to be
brighter,

As the sleep gets thinner, dreams should be the
pacifier,
It's alright to have nightmares, just keep that
aplomb burning, that's your fire,

Sometimes life can be avidly baffling, live it,
learn it, the plan is to lift you higher,
Look around, look within, it's all hues of hope,
be a humble buyer,

Dusk of fear, failure, and fatigue come with the
package, but you got to beat them to see that
dawn of desire,

Be kind, be brave, belittle the pessimism, write
your own story instead of living a satire,

Manifest courage, cultivate faith, happily pursue
what you aspire,
Hone your craft, make it large, it will all pay off,
the sacrifice and the perspire,
The world is becoming meaner as times get dire,
But you be wise; choose the truth, irony is they
might still call you a liar,

And all that pulls you down won't matter once
you rise beyond and higher,
While water keeps gushing, something stays
forever, be that Pier.

Lighthouse

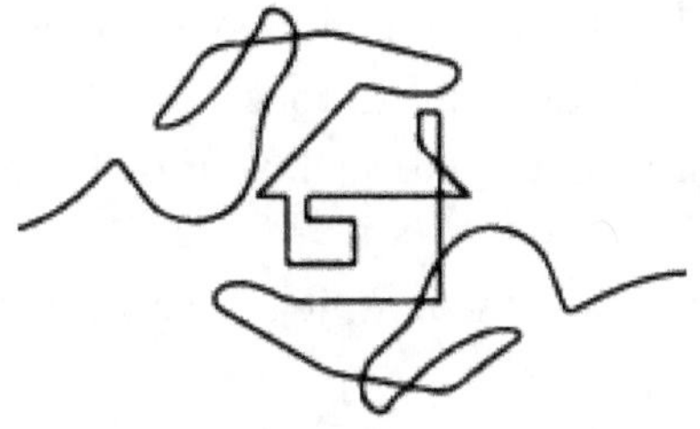

Unknown is to travel like river is for gravels,
You are curious, you are cleansed,
You discover faith, you unravel.

For bedrock may be a low point, and then sharks
may blabber,
You still shoot for the moon,
Put in all you got, all you have known, for the
unknown is also like Scrabble.

And while to swim may be an art, but to float on
the brim is peace; that's my chapel,
Freely follow the sun glint on water,
Let it be your guide, your friend, your saddle.

Inhibitions, prohibitions, will try to cage you,
the exhibition of worldly shackles,
For what it's worth,

You be you, the child that used to roar, roam,
and crackle.

Life and its hassle, sometimes you cannot tackle,
You may always hope to cope,
For your dreams, your soul, your will is your
straddle.
Bit by bit, blow by blow, it gets beautiful, this
battle,
Be humble, for even if you stumble,
Try and use that fall as your paddle.

For the unknown is to travel…

Petals

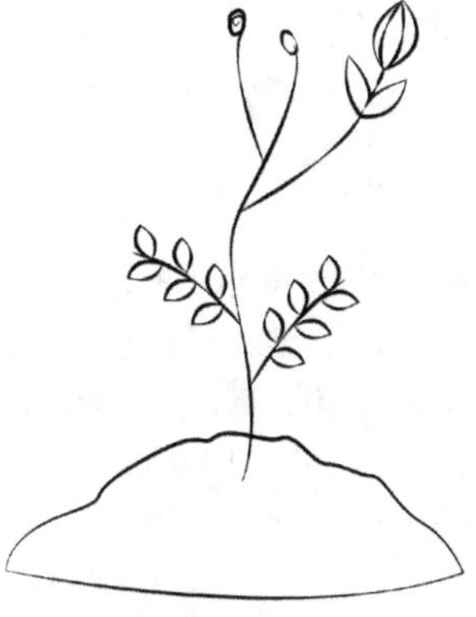

Garner learnings from the past,
Mold it into a beautiful cast,
Observe and absorb, slow the fast,
Be humble, be humane; let that be your mast.

In the sea of life, learn to float you learn to
survive, learn to swim you learn to succeed,
Along with care and nourishment, it's the mud
and the heat that grow the seed,
They coexist – the vice and the wise, the hope
and the disguise, choice is yours whom to feed,
Being kind is the new strong; let there be light
and let love take the lead.

Hug your dreams with hope and zeal, be a
go-getter,
Be good, and it will be better,
Hold onto yourself, no matter what, do not deter,
Do good; karma is the postman for spirit and
letter.

Journey is just a fraction of a dot to pass,
Where there is no first, no last,
But lots of thrill, frills, lessons, and class,
So, make the most of it; life is an art, make it
vast.

What needs you is all you need,
It is meant to be yours, don't even have to plead,
Attend your calling, don't let it be eclipsed by
greed,
Be altruistic, rank we over me, that way you will
feel freed.

Year after year, it's not like a score/tab you got to
settle,
You with all your ingredients are amazing; live
it, pour it out of the kettle,
And there will be storms, face them, go show
your mettle,
The story of every mighty sequoia started with a
tiny petal!!

Felicity

It's not dark, if you hope for light,
It's not loss, if you still putting up that fight.

It's not a home run, if you are not running for the
team,
It's not over, if you still have (even) one
unfulfilled dream.

It's not a scar, if you still believe in your wishing
star,
It's not success, if you and you are still at war.

It's not art, if it is not coming from the heart,
It's not passion, if you know the end but don't
know where to start.

It's not a song, if you sing it with doubt,
It's not heard, if it's all noise and no worthy
shout.

It's not humane, if someone somewhere is still in
pain,
It's not just, if irrespective of caste, creed,
gender, religion, collar, everyone is not treated
equally and same.
It's not true, if it needs different versions of you,
It's not destined, if in the process, you can't find
you.

Tunnel Song

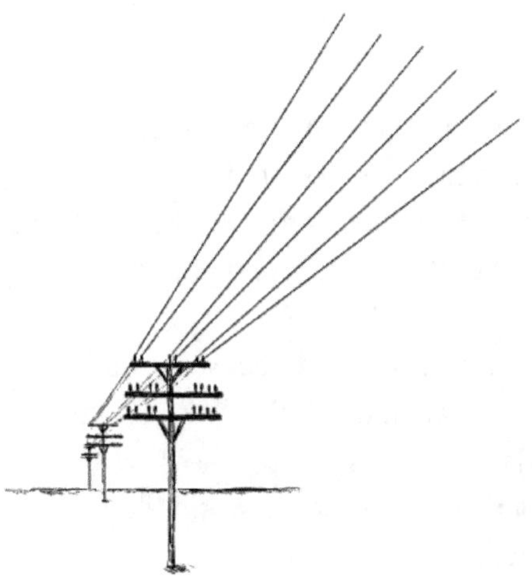

Not everyone helps you when you are down,
But that is how you know you are moving close
to the crown.

You might break a little when others make fun
while you frown,
But you got to realize inside you lies your happy
town.

They are not friends, if they leave you to drown,
And they are family when they make sure to
you, you are found!

Sometimes the whole world might seem upside
down,
It's during those times, you need to hold your
ground.

You don't need to shout to be heard, sometimes
silence is the strongest sound,
Smiles and memories matter, they make you feel
way richer than dollars and pound.

We fear, we love, we hope, we inspire, we are
humans if we don't do those, we are just wild
hounds,
Be yourself in this poker world, don't get
clowned.

Lost in the cogwheel where we seem to enjoy
even though we are bound,
Sometimes, breaking free, falling off the radar,
is necessary to (re)live that merry-go-round.

Fireflies

When life gets bizarre,
I turn to my dream jar.

How it all started, the story of the spark,
From Twinkly Star to that Hot Wheels car,
From Galaxy bars to my Givson guitar,

It's incredible to have come this far.

From those wounds and their scars,
From turning those scars into my trademark,
Walking through them storms, anchoring myself
a spar,

It's a panacea to have these life lessons in my jar.

From a head full of doubts to an undaunted
heart,
From all kinds of chaos to hold on to the gutsy
Mozart,

Picking up the losses, blows, and bedrocks to
weave them into a bard,

It feels good to be human amongst them worldly
Czars.
And it's alright to sway a bit in this beautiful
ballpark,
But remember to resurrect, because you are your
(only) own shooting star,
For what it's worth, keep dreaming, keep
fighting, keep hoping, battle by battle, and you
will Win your War,

Be the lamp that reigned the dark.

And whenever life gets bizarre,
Well, just count them as fireflies and
Turn them into your dream jar!!

Javelin

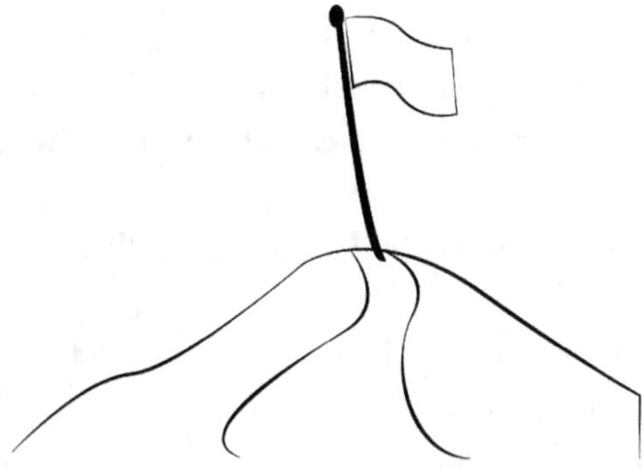

More you grind, more it gets better,
That's true for life, just like for cake's batter.

Go innocently wild, have a poetic ride, dream
big, speak of joy and vigor and faith,
Universe listens to every black and white
chatter.

Be rich from heart, be umpteen in kindness, be
we before I,
More you give, more is there for everyone,
radiate light and let it scatter.

How brave you are, lies in seeing the storm in
the eye, lies in hoping when it's aching,

It's humane to fail, to feel pain, but choose
courage and let it be your anchor.

And sometimes things might shatter,
Collect those pieces, make art out of it,
That's a marvel; it's not easy, but worth a flatter.

The ones doubting you, they are just there for
the chatter,
If you know yourself, you believe in yourself,
you will rise and shine,
That is all that matter.

Just like a javelin, push yourself harder, higher,
better, and farther,
Hold firm, have faith and run, run like a panther,
Unleash yourself, let that release be your mentor.

Word Game!

Sometimes it's only words,

When things go berserk,
When you offer but don't get served,
When chaos becomes mood of the earth,
When hope seems to be the only, yet the greatest
perk,
When in the Carnival of Rust, emotions take a
burp.
Sometimes it's only words!!

When you can unconditionally create happiness,
that makes a strong verse,
When someone counts on you, that is the real
treasure, one to keep safe in life's purse,

When you seek from outside, but actually it's the
inside that needs to be searched,
When you are committed enough to put yourself
through it, for what it's worth,
When you try, fail, try, repeat till the efforts and
your calling merge,
Sometimes it's only words!!

When you lose a match or two but go on to win
the tournament because that's the plan of the
universe,
When you keep climbing, but the top keeps
getting taller, it's not you are getting smaller
rather you keep growing better, observe,
When divides and agendas keep running through
the world, humanity more than ever needs to
hold its nerve,
When amongst the intellectuals, the wise remain
in dearth,
When good in one another must be seen, to
make it one better, brighter, braver hearth!!

It is times like these, when it's only words but
are mightier than a thousand swords!!

Invictus

If it's a loop, break it, don't make it,
World has gone for a toss, but there is still a lot
of good, take it!

Cannot understand the brutality, leave it,
Can understand humanity, weave it!

Divide and (just) survive, while together we all
can thrive; tough choice?
It will be either a requiem of a saga or it will be
a tale where people used to love, laugh, and
rejoice!

Bad days happen, good days are made, hold
them,
So many flavours, so many fireworks, so many
dreams–you are, unfold them!

For some it's written in the stars, while for some
it's written in their scars, read them,
From dusk to dawn, from zeal to zeon, it's all in
you, lead them!

Hope is abundant, but it's a conquest, who is for
the taking?
Be real, be you, fun part is, a lot of souls don't
even know why they are faking!

It won't be easy, no, but it will be worth it, fight
it,
Use your falls as your climb, use your passion,
as your shine, ignite it, go light it!

Talk, be helpful, be kind to someone, anyone,
everyone, embrace it,
Each one of us is magical, need is to trace it,
grace it!

If Only

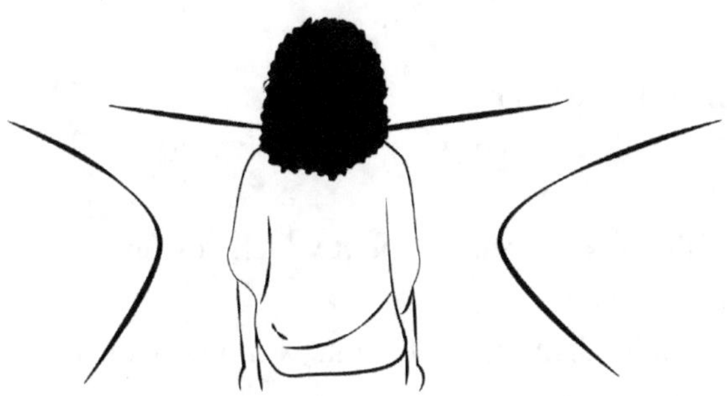

If you choose to be strong,
You will be your own war song.

If you decide to not give up,
You will grow with every hiccup.

If you believe in yourself,
80% of the battle is already dealt.

If amidst chaos you stay humble,
You will be a soothing oak in the middle of a
jungle.

If you hold on to hope,
You will walk beautifully on life's tightrope.

If you dream and don't sleep on it,
Slowly, steadily, you will be the tortoise who
won it.

If you face your fears,
You will see who stays and who spears.

If there is something about which you are
passionate,
Then let them throw lemons, you know the trick
to make lemonade.
If you hold your post when it's raining fiascos,
You will learn to dance the storm de facto.

If you say as you see,
You may lose, but you will be free.

If you can pray,
You won't sway.

If you not only think about a better world but act
to make the world better,
On judgement day, you will be known as a
go-getter.

If the stars and moon still bring you delight,
Then no matter how dark it gets, the night, you
will still find your light!!

Fireworks

What is there to hold back,
What is there to hold back,

Happy or sad,
We do carry our sacks.
To hope is to heal,
If we are living that, then we are leaving
beautiful tracks.
Strength lies in staying when everything is
swaying,
If you grind in the sun, no night is ever going to
be black;
What is there to hold back?

No matter what, the best version of you, you
should manifest,
Why crib when you can stitch your cracks,
Your struggle, your story, your guts, your glory,
Life may be an open source, but it doesn't come
with hacks.
Be a giver, be the reason for someone,
Be a wildflower amongst the wolf packs;
What is there to hold back?

Do what you feel, for whom you feel,
With your head held high, walk through the
worldly quacks,
Lit a dream, keep it burning,
Sculpt some beautiful memories in life's stack,
Try, Try, Keep trying for what it's worth,
Live, love, laugh, light up, while advancing
through the life traps.
After all, What is there to hold back!!

Rise

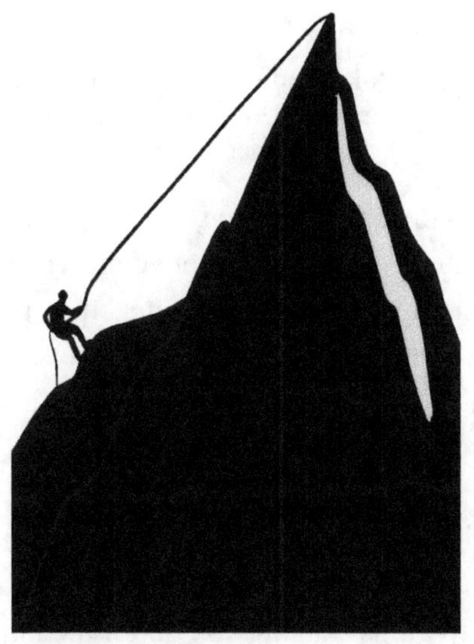

It's about the steps you take,
Because they'll define the path you make.
What you are running away from is chasing you,
Better look it in the face and prove your mettle,
quit escape.

And it is all right to break,
After all, the world ain't itself in a proper place.
There can always be a U-turn, one can always
restart,
Just ensure, amidst all the hustle and bustle,
peace (humanity) has the highest stake.

But after that despicable sleep, you got to wake,
And put in all you got–the serenity and the rage.
Let them make fun, let them doubt it,
You don't partake, remember, you are meant to
be great.

No one can slow your pace,
Once you have decided to set your own stage.
For men may come and characters may go,
But you get a standing ovation from everyone,
(including yourself), play your part in such a
way!

In the deck of life, you are your best card,
Trick is to play it with utmost grit and glaze.
They say life is a game, you go for the brace,
Stay hopeful, stay (with) you! that's your glory,
that's your grace.

Because in the end you will be remembered
either as the one who arrived late,
Or the one who tried and tried and wrote his/her
own slate.
Live, learn, love, laugh, lead, laud,
Be the knight who lights up the world into a
bigger, better, and brighter day when the nights
fade!

Wabi Sabi

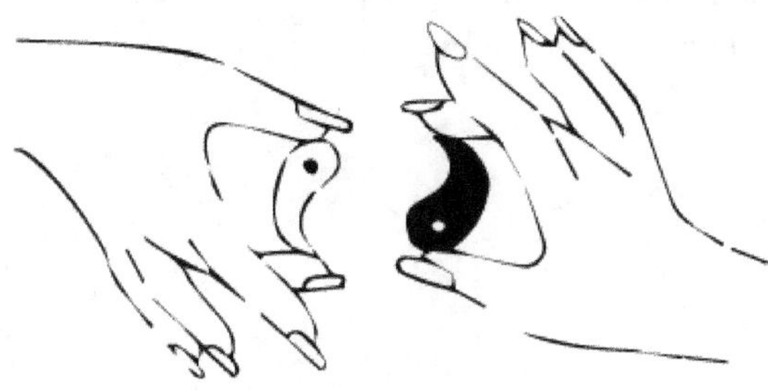

It is as important to remember your war cry
during the battle as it is before the battle starts,

The sky may be full of clouds, pouring down
storms and whatnot, it's important to remember
the same sky is full of stars.

For the waters may be testing, and when you see
a high tide, remember, sometimes you are
bounced up just to go past them, lurking sharks,

When it's cold outside and dews turn frosty,
hearten yourself, remember, dreams can always
be worn as scarf.

When things don't go your way, which often
might be the case, remember to hope, for hope is
such a spark, it made Tony a Stark.

Be home to your wounds, don't fight them, but
win them, remember if the world is Hogwarts,
you will be known by your scar.

Show Must Go On

The tunnel may be dark and deep,
Tough times may turn all wisdom bleak,
You may end up at the opposite end of what you
seek,

Then be your own war song, for the
Show must go on.

In a cobweb of socialites, be a giver,
Despite losing, if you can help someone win,
that's your shimmer,
And on the pitch of life, world will bamboozle
you every now and then with that odd beamer,

Then hold tight and keep swinging, for the
Show must go on.

Travel, to get closer to yourself, to discover
yourself,
It's not about the destination, but the journey and
the hiccups and the bumps en route and how you
dealt,
Adapt to adept in every situation, with every
person, for every reason, be organic, be off the
shelf,

Be the silver lining amidst gloomy clouds, for
the
Show must go on.

Some call it failure, some call it loss, some get
hurt, while some call it just bad luck,
But with passion for your cause and a little bit of
introspective pause, fortune is all yours to pluck,
During highs, you have the entourage; during
lows, it's all about passing the buck,

However, you be candidly brave and aspire to
inspire, for the
Show must go on.

Postcard

At night, what shines is called a star,
In life, what helps you shine is called a scar.

In music, what adds rock to it is called guitar,
In disguise, if you can still be the rock, you are
called Mozart.

When in power, everyone reigns, call it Czar,
When in pain, still hope to reign, call it Stark.

Stains on white sheets get super visible, darker
ones seldom get mar,

In a world full of versions, be brave to be who
you are.

Keep living same day, same way forever, that is
putting life in a jar,
Make mistakes, learn, travel, write, read, live, at
times be bizarre.

In inner world, with closed eyes, what may seem
so close, in real world it's called far,
So better keep your dreams close and hope
closer, everything is reachable once you set it on
heart's radar.

Pick some

For some it's a bed of roses, for some it's a
cakewalk,
For some it's an uphill battle, for some it's a
kimura lock,
And both 'some' may end up having the same
outcome,
But one wins the game, and one wins the heart.

For some may choose ambitions, for some may
be power-driven,
For some may choose compassion, for some
may be on a humble mission,
Both 'some' may excel on their turf,
But one chooses to rule, while the other is
chosen to serve.

For some may hearsay, for some may slay,
For some may obey, for some may pray,
Both 'some' feel they are right,
But one is a flaunter, and one is a fighter.

For some may dodge, for some may escape,
For some may dab, for some may face,
Both 'some' may get away,
But one leaves the scene, and one lives the
dream.

For some may shout, for some may announce,
For some may work in silence, for some may
astound,
Both 'some' mean business,
But one relies too much on sound, and one aims
to be found.

For some use tricks, for some use sticks,
For some may fail and learn to fix, for some may
fall and rise above all hicks,
Both 'some' may succeed,
But one is hollow, and the other is valour.

For some through power, for some show power,
For some earn power, for some grace power,
Both 'some' believe they are strong,
But one is a short-lived song, while the other is
to stay long, undisputed like King Kong.

For some, for some,
But one, and the other–won!

Sonder

I see light when I see someone fight,
For what's worth, for what's right,

When love binds, when words rhyme,
When kindness shines, I see a diamond in dark
mine,

Where peace rest, where inspiration is at its best,
Where with care we weave humanity's nest, is
where I see passion passing life's toughest test,

With respect for each other's story, With
admiration for nature's upholstery,
With accompanying one another in unraveling
life's mystery, I see our ultimate glory,

To go through the low, to grow through the
show,

To learn to be the water, and at times to be the
boat both, I see true meaning of Hope.

Rising with hope, hugging your thoughts,
Having courage to see past your fears, I see
dreams sprouting to life.

Bits and Pieces

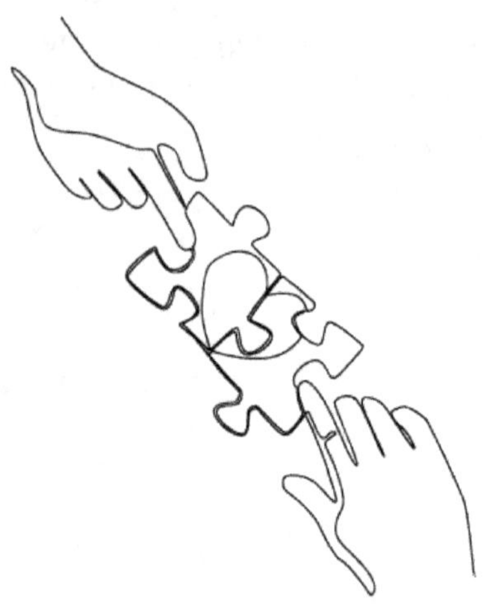

You face it,

Because if you face it, you grace it.
Either life can startle you, or you can amaze it.
Choice is yours, sell it or take it.

To the ones you matter, it's enough, to others, it
won't ever be, so you better be you and ace it.
The biggest dare is to share, to care, to be fair,
and not to fake it.
At times you got to be Bolt, at times the
Tortoise, race is not just to win it, but to live it,
celebrate it.

When feeling lost, look within, what you see
(find), go chase it.
Keep building your castle, for there will be
blows and storms to shake it.
Rest yourself in hope, no matter what, you will
make it.

The batter may be perfectly mixed with all the
ingredients and cherries and cocoa, but you get
the real deal only when you bake it,
Just like in life, you may have all the talent,
super skills, still to prove your mettle, you got to
quake it,
Peace is the new power, serene is the new
success, all the malices, them vices we see, force
lies within us to break it.

Scars to stars, your struggle, your story, your
glory, own it. Embrace it.
Be humble, be kind, be more, that's the magic
trick to glace it.
And at some point, in time, lights are going to
go dim, have faith and it will pass, but you got to
face it,

Because if you face it, you grace it.

Symphony

At times in life, you got to Honk,
Yes! Not to others but to yourself,
To your dream, to your instincts, to your belief,
to your passion, to your art,
Not one, or twice but as many times as needed to
hit the bull's eye on life's dart,
You go to Honk, for the show must have some
pomp.

At times in life, you got to hold back,
For you are the creation of the divine,
Hold back them voices in your head, hold back
them whispers in your mind, hold back
everything and anything that doubts the element
of divine,
While wishing through them shooting stars,
struggles are thy real shooting stars, keep in
mind.

You got to hold back, to let go off that sack, to
indent a happy track.

At times in life, you got to go with the flow,
Be like water and mould your way through,
With the crest and the trough, the solitude and
the gratitude, the blues, and the hues,
Being avidly open to them changes and the
challenges, enjoying the ebb and the flow,
You got to go with the flow, let them tolls add to
the glow.

At times in life, you got to dance in the rain,
Knowledge, knead, and kindness never go in
vain,
Have a song for the storms, face your fears, and
grow strong; no matter how difficult the yard is,
one can always stomp,
Wearing the coat of wit, holding the umbrella of
grit, taking leaps of will and faith,
Do dance in the rain, for if only one is humane,
one can earn his/her claim.

Many a time in life you got to celebrate,
Cherish and relish them little perks it offers
every now and then,
Be it the amazing family, incredible friends,
shimmery dreams, or ineffable God's plan,

Listen to your heart, speak to your mind, yolo,
and it's most beautiful when you are the looker,
and you are the find.
Celebrate the symphonies of life, rise above it
all, never hesitate to feel great.

Resurrection

Life may not always be fair,
For sometimes decisions you've made may bring
despair,
But then all hope should never be lost,
For the ones who still count on you, you are
their glow, you are their glare.

You may have lost a battle or two,
For sometimes you may have been dragged into
a dungeon you have no clue,
But then you must garner all your strength,
For in the end, either one will win, You and your
blues or You and your Hues.

It may be dark and gloomy, not only them days
but also in the heart,
For sometimes you may feel damn where and
when should I Start,
But it's never too late till you can see that dream,
For if you trust your art, even in disguise, you
shall be a Mozart.

Your friends, your foes, your fights, your blows,
your highs, your lows are upskilling you,
For sometimes you may look in the mirror and
say to that man–what did I do to deserve you,
But that is the time to have faith in yourself, in
your dreams, your hopes, and your tryst,
For you all have made it this far & with a little
bit of faith, you will sail through.

You must sail through.

Hymn for Hope

Every tunnel comes with two choices,
Retreat or Ride,
Because sometimes in life it's about the fight and
not about the prize.

It's your stage, it's your show, and there will be
times when it's all dim, no light,
Well, go steal some, feel some, zeal some,
Remember, the only goal is you; paint it bright.

These are the cards life has dealt; you can either
play or plight,
Fear or Faith, your pick, one of them definitely
has a greater height.

So, what if it's a fall, take it with full pride, let it
escort you to your flight,
It's in the unseen, the uncertain, the unspoken,
you got to keep your dreams in sight.

If 'today' did not work out, what matters is what
you do 'tonight',
'Tomorrow' is defined by both, so set it right,

For sometimes you let loose, sometimes you
buckle up, sit tight,
But the plan is to seek with each hide and grow
with each glide.

You lose some, you learn some, even if you
don't win some, never shy to strive,
After all, it's not a lab; you are not walking out
with results; it's life, and you always walk out
with Life.

SupeHum

Wear the cape of kindness
Fly on wings of faith
Life will throw an odd ball every now and then
Play your best shot, for what it's worth it.

Hold on to the rope of hope
Try and make everyone feel special
For life should be large and beautiful
Even in tough times, just sonder

Be yourself, no matter how hard it is or scared
you are
Be someone who tries to make a difference
After all, world ain't itself in perfect shape
Keep believing in Good

In times of being viral
If you can be, be humble
In times of superheroes
If you can be, be humane

Road is long, full of bumps and shocks
But you are strong, living your own version of
Forest Gump and
Hancock
Being human is the new superhero
Be one and Voila!

Better, in spirit, and in letter…

Whatever pulls you down, You better keep
doing,
It all adds to the taste, (even if it's bitter for now)
You better keep brewing.
Bits and blitz, and grit and glitz, and bolts and
blows,
You better keep sewing,
Each of the above pieces is a master, making the
story a masterpiece,
You better keep glowing through whatever you
are going.
Pursue your passion with all the wit and will,
and when you reach there, remember–

When you start getting, You better keep giving,
Be kind, help some, if you could be hope for
some,
That's the difference between being alive and
living. You better keep living.
Best shot is not the one hit hardest, but a touch
of technique and finesse,
You better keep timing,
Bitcoins and crypto may be trending, but being
human is invaluably unmeasurable, it's worth it,
You better keep mining.
Sounds of joy, coy, ploy, annoy, and whatnot,
World keeps singing,
Jab by jab and Hook by hook, don't retreat,
You better keep swinging.
In the ledger of life, there will be all kinds of
days, and there will be a knight,
You better keep shining,
Through the storms, soaring above them clouds,
You better be that silver lining.
You fail, you fall, you learn, you ball in times–
tense and fragile,
You better keep walling,
You look, you search, you save, you purge, to
figure it out,
You better keep calling.

Gifts

Dawn says bring it on, I will be ready,
I made it through the storm, I am strong.
Dewy mornings sing those hopeful hymns,
For sky is to fly, let love and courage be thy
wings.
Noon says after that hustle and bustle, kindly
rest,
Pause, introspect, and resurrect; whatever
happens, happens for the best.

Evening says let's rejoice, for all the wonderful
things in life,
With family, friends, and near and dear ones,
let's make the most of this ride.
Twilight reflects the scarlet complexities,
Inspire to find one's purpose amongst them
perplexities.
Dusk soothes the palpable mind,
Gentle breeze of wind on the face says it's worth
it, (to) keep trying.
Night comes with all its stars and moon and
rhymes,
Gives us a gift, for we got all that we need to
rise and shine.

Questions

Stormy night exists,
Only till you see the daylight,
Do you see the daylight?
Scorching heat pains,
Only till you find the rain,
Did you find the rain?
The climb mocks,
Only till you reach the top,
Did you reach the top?
Doubts eclipse hope,
Only till you have faith to cope,
Do you have faith?

And these are not worldly battles to fight,
Rather, it's all within, because,
You are the Daylight, You are the Rain,
You are the Top, You are the Faith,
It's all in you, the path and the destination,
It is all you and for you to take.
Purpose is missing,
Only till you attend your calling,
What's your calling?
Magic perishes,
Only till you dream about something and cherish
it,
How lucidly you dream?
Courage retreats,
Only till you show you cannot give up, won't
give up despite all the cheats and the beats,
Can you show that?
Burden is heavy,
Only till you learn to float and don't let levy,
Why to float?
For what may seem impossible at the start,
Maybe the only distance between ? and !,
Call your dreams, show them no matter what
you won't give up,

And when it gets too heavy, learn to drop it, to
crop it, to rock it, and that's how you remain
afloat.

For you are the sail, you are the storm, you are
the anchor, and you are the Boat!!

Let's try!

Sometimes you choose, and sometimes it's
chosen for you,
Learn to grow, accept, and absorb the blow and
the boo,
For without them wounds and scars,
The story will be like a star with no hue.
Ignite the fire, let them flames erupt higher,
Stay humble, focus on what you deserve rather
than what you desire,
For this world is one beautiful place to be,
Only if you have some worthy dreams to hire.
Shy not from failing, fusing, fading, or facing,

All the flavours are for the taking, keep gracing,
That's the recipe for a delightful dish,
At times sweet, at times salty, at times sour, or at
times tangy, but you keep embracing.
Lead by your deeds, stay by your words,
Still, there will be someone always throwing
dirt,
You keep moving, avidly scrubbing,
As they may not, but you know your weight, you
know your worth.
See around you, help some, be there for some,
It's due to our Karma, we become what we
become,
Life can be awfully baffling at times with all its
temptations and offerings,
Keep what you need and share what you keep,
do justice to the crown you wear called Human.

www.ingramcontent.com/pod-product-compliance
Lightning Source LLC
La Vergne TN
LVHW050932200726
843508LV00011B/2329